ANIMAL FACES

By Akira Satoh (photos) and Kyoko Toda (text)
Translated by Amanda Mayer Stinchecum

Kane/Miller Book Publishers

A C U R I O U S N E L L B O O K

First American Edition 1996 by Kane/Miller Book Publishers
Brooklyn, New York & La Jolla, California

Originally published in Japan under the title *Minna No Kao* (*Animals' Faces*)
by Fukuinkan Shoten, Publishers Inc., Tokyo, 1994

For information contact:
Kane/Miller Book Publishers
P.O. Box 310529, Brooklyn, N.Y. 11231-0529.

Library of Congress Catalog Card Number 95-81578
ISBN 0-916291-62-6

Book designed by Shinbo Minami
Printed and bound in Japan
1 2 3 4 5 6 7 8 9 10

INTRODUCTION

This is a book about observation—close observation. That means looking at things very carefully so that you are able to see the differences between things that upon first glance look exactly alike.

In this book you will be looking at photographs of animal faces, which for a particular species of animal you might expect to look very much alike. But, in fact, for each of the 24 species of animals included in this book, each one of the 21 photos for that animal shows a different face. It is up to you to look at seemingly identical faces and then to discover how they all differ from each other. This is the same as looking at a group of people who at first may look alike, but upon closer observation look very different from each other—in fact, look highly individual.

It is your job to figure out how each face differs from every other one, by its markings, shape, color or expressiveness. And then it will be your job to apply these observation skills when looking at other things that you encounter in your daily life. Have fun.

CONTENTS

GORILLA

The gorilla is the largest member of the primate family. Although
gorillas are very strong, they're also very sensitive. If startled
or worried by something, they sometimes get a stomachache.
So if you see a gorilla napping at the zoo, just watch quietly.
You don't want to cause any stomachaches.
Do any of these gorillas look worried to you?

CAMEL

Have you ever looked at camels' teeth? They're made for biting off tough grass and then very slowly grinding it down. When you visit the zoo, wait for a camel to open its mouth and take a look. You'll see what we mean.
Which of these camels could use braces on their teeth?

LESSER PANDA

The lesser panda loves to run around its play area in the zoo.
If you watch carefully, you'll see it rub its behind on rocks
and trees. The lesser panda does this to leave its
smell wherever it goes. This makes it feel comfortable, as if
to say, "This is my territory, so keep off."
Which of these look as if they're guarding their space?

ELEPHANT

The elephant is the largest land animal. When happy, sad or angry, elephants express their feelings with their big bodies and long trunks. Look and you'll see that even their eyes and ears are saying something! If you observe them closely, you too will be able to understand the elephants' feelings. Can you find the happy, sad or angry elephants?

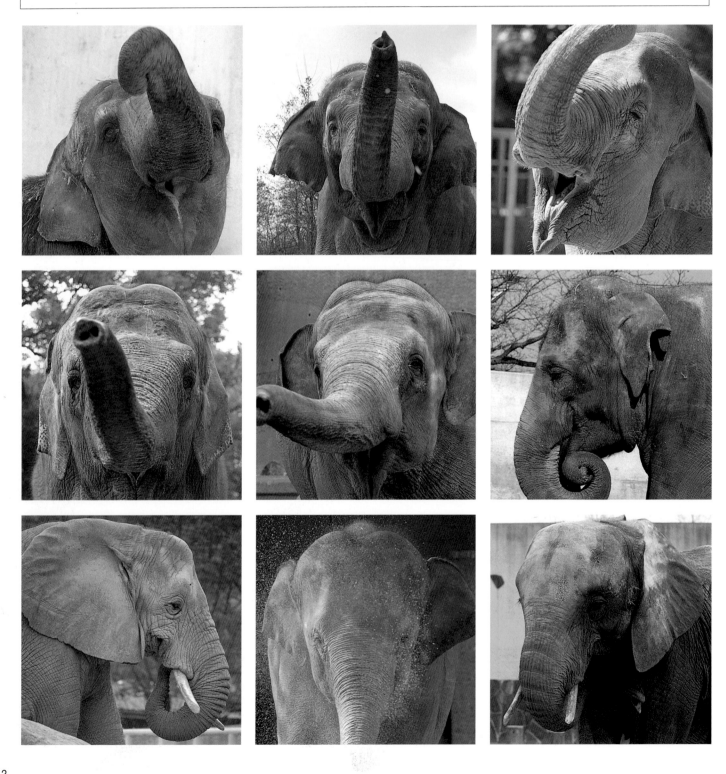

SEAL

Seals are full of curiosity. They'll stick their faces out
of the water to watch you as you come near them at the zoo.
Maybe even the wild seals that live near the shore are
looking at people from the sea. What do you think these seals
would be saying if they could talk to you?

R H I N O C E R O S

Look at the ears of the rhinoceros. The rhinoceros
can move them any way it likes, twitching them in every
direction. In this way it can hear sounds from the front,
from behind and even sounds from far away.
What do you think their ears look like?

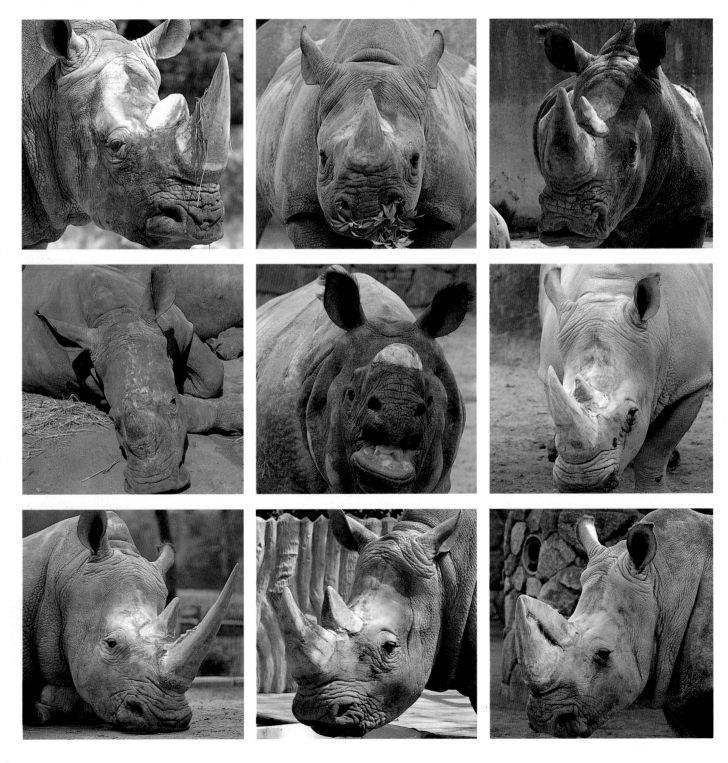

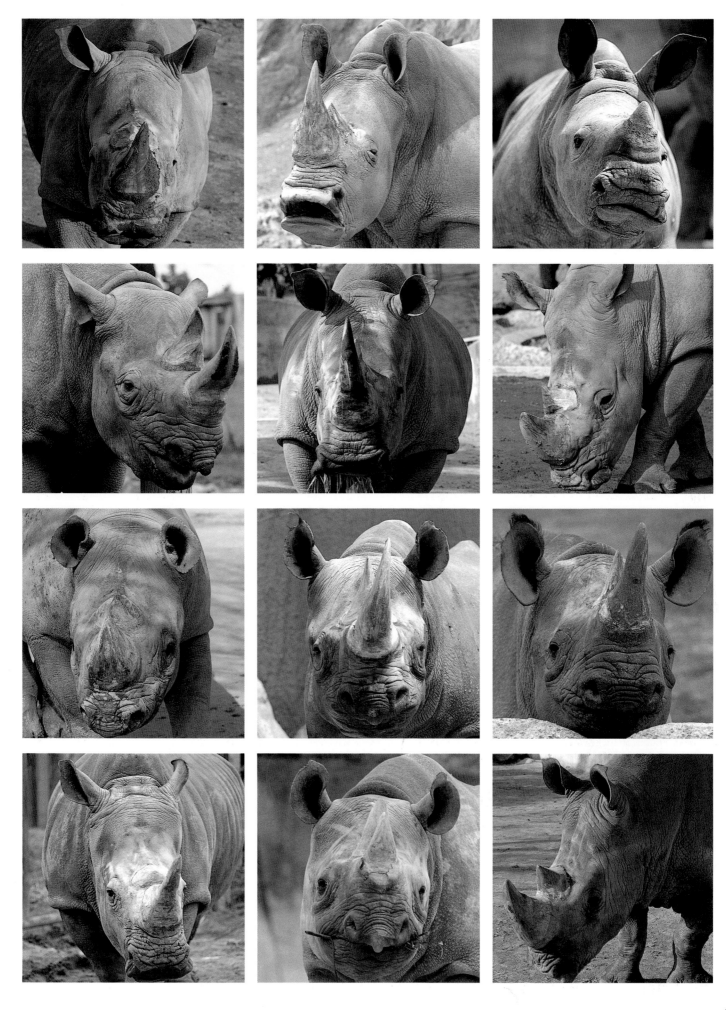

OTTER

Otters are expert swimmers. But they hate getting wet!
When they get out of the water, they will dry themselves
off by rubbing against grass or cloth. Can you tell which of
these have just come out of the water?

POLAR BEAR

Polar bears like the winter cold. They're not at all crazy about summer heat. All they do in warm weather is stay in the water and swim around. The polar bear's fur actually changes from winter to summer. In the winter, it's pure white and beautiful. But in the summer, they shed their fur, and it looks all mottled. By looking at their fur, can you tell what season it is?

RACCOON DOG

The raccoon dog is native to Japan. It makes its home in
the forests and hills, but as people put up houses and build roads
in those parts, it has fewer and fewer places to live.
Almost all the raccoon dogs in Japanese zoos were brought there
because they had either been hit by cars or had lost their homes.
How can you tell one raccoon dog from another?

TAPIR

The tapir does nothing but sleep.
It loves taking naps!
Be careful if a tapir wakes up and shows you its behind.
That could mean it's about to pee in your direction.
Which of these tapirs look sleepy?

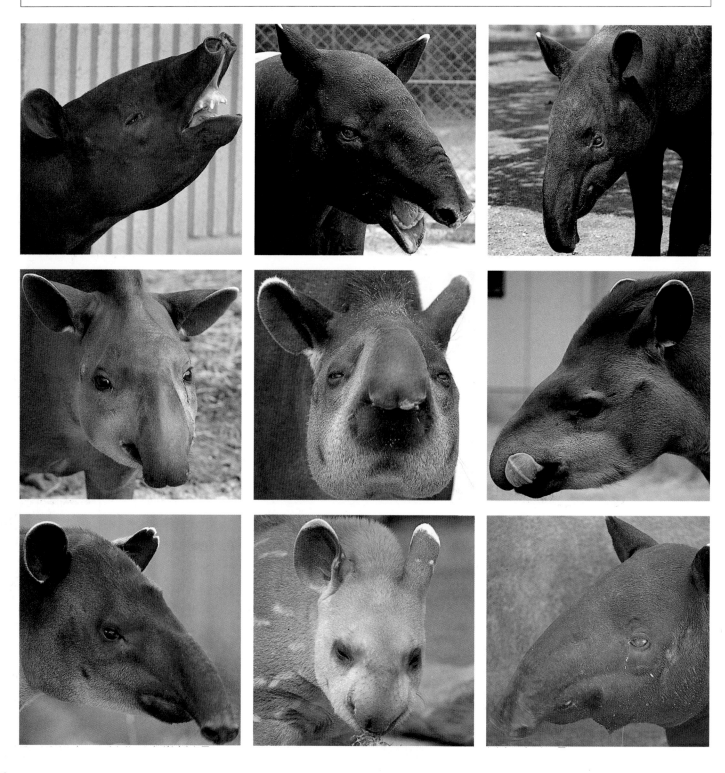

GOAT

Most goats like to be petted, and when scratched behind
the ears, they actually seem quite happy. But there are some
goats who would rather be left alone and not petted.
Maybe it's just a matter of enjoying their own company.
Which of these goats would you like to scratch behind the ears?

ORANGUTAN

The orangutan works at things very slowly but patiently.
It could work all day at tearing up the grass or overturning
a huge stone in its play area at the zoo. Zoo-keepers never
cease to be amazed at the persistence of the orangutan.
Can you spot the orangutans who look ready for mischief?

TIGER

Tigers are members of the cat family. If you watch them
carefully—the way they drink, eat or even the way they
rub their backs on the ground, you'll see they act exactly like
house cats. The patterns on their faces vary.
Can you tell one tiger from another by its stripes?

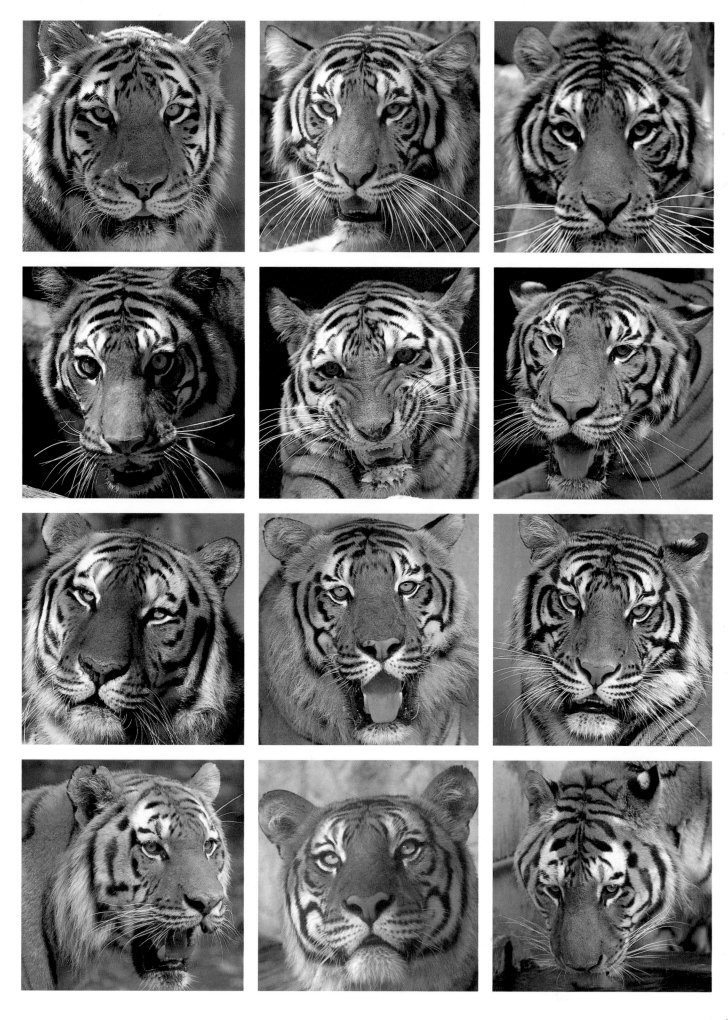

KANGAROO

Kangaroos don't like loud noises.
To avoid them, babies hide in their mothers' pouches.
Big ones just run away.
When you watch kangaroos at the zoo, do it quietly.
Do any of these kangaroos look startled?

HIPPOPOTAMUS

The hippopotamus is a master at submerging itself under water. Even a newborn hippo is able to stay under water. If you do spot some under water in a pool, take a good look. The length of time they can stay under water is different for each one. Do you have a favorite hippo face on these pages?

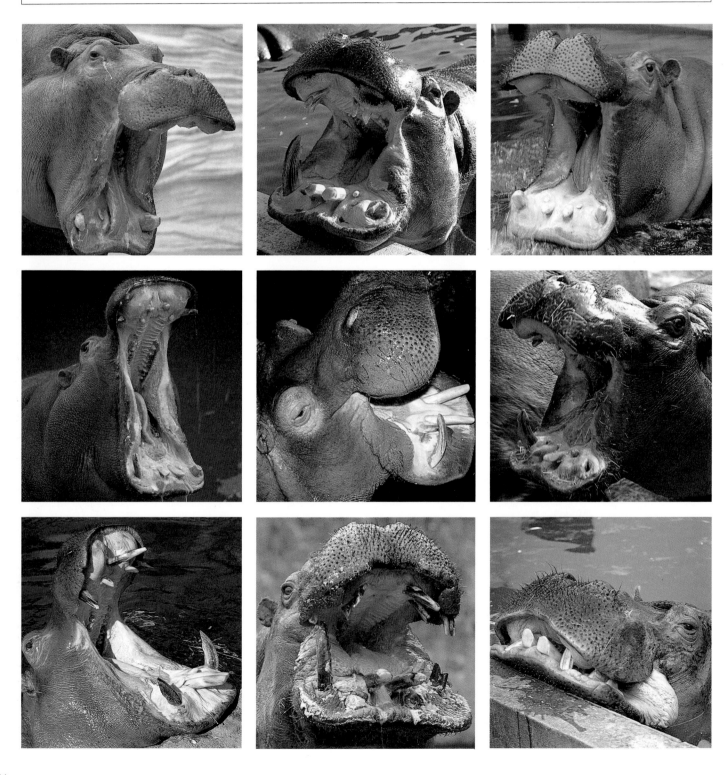

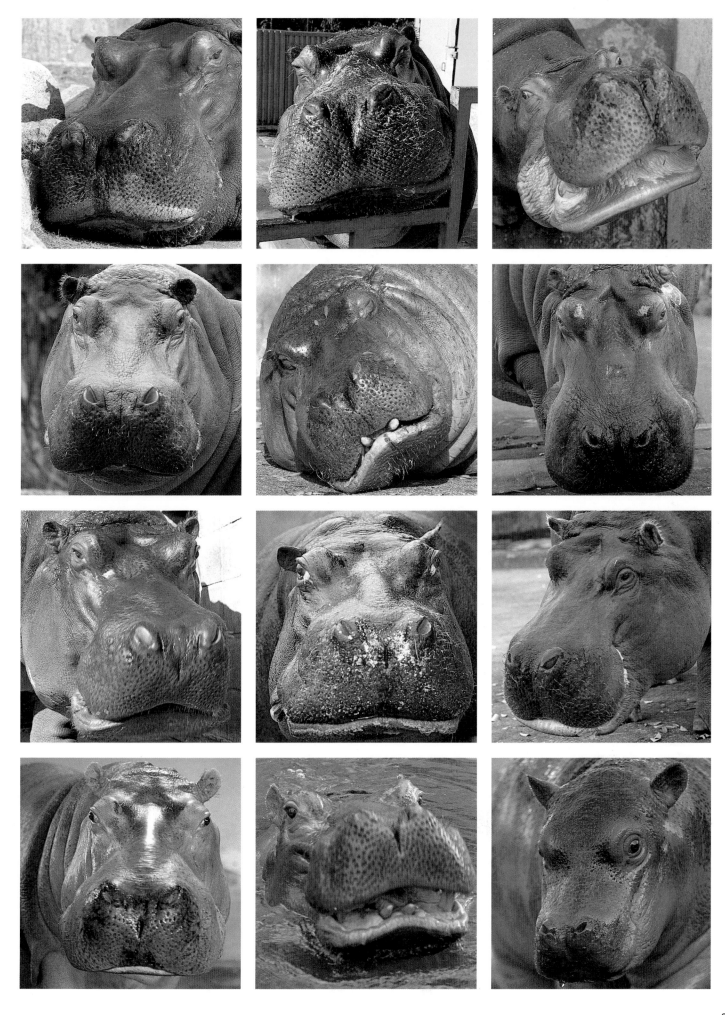

ASIATIC BLACK BEAR

The Asiatic black bear, recognizable by its distinctive white collar,
lives in the mountains of Japan as well as other countries.
But now, because people have moved into mountain areas, this bear
has few places left to live. If the human population continues to
spread, the only home left for the Asiatic black bear will be zoos.
How many white collars can you actually see?

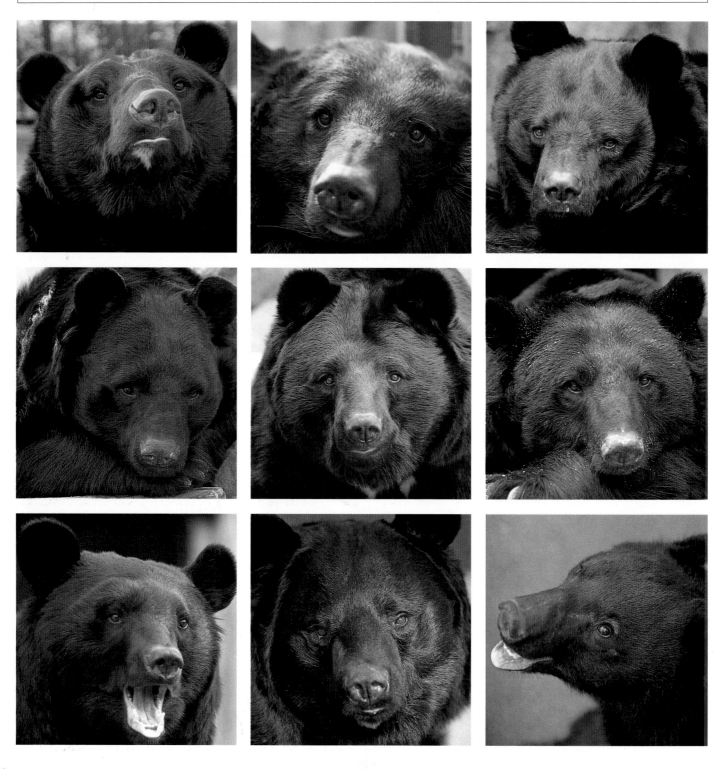

CHIMPANZEE

Chimpanzees like to tease people who come to the zoo to look at them. They may throw things or even spit. Of course, they learned these "tricks" by mimicking people. So, you might want to think twice about how you behave, in case you give the chimps some bad ideas. Does it look as though any of these chimps are ready to throw something?

GIRAFFE

At the zoo you can watch the giraffe eating the leaves of tall trees. It stretches its long tongue out to reach the leaves, wraps it around them and then pulls the leaves back into its mouth. Giraffes living in the wilds of Africa eat leaves from trees the same way. What helps you tell one giraffe face from another?

WOLF

Wolves once lived in many more countries than they do today. In Japan, for instance, they were thought to be dangerous animals, so people killed off all the wolves. Today in Japan, the only place you'll see wolves is in a zoo, and those had to be brought from zoos in other countries. All around the world there are fewer and fewer forests left where wolves still live. Do these wolves look especially dangerous to you?

FOX

Even at the zoo the fox is often invisible, hiding in high grass or in a hole. But if you stand still and wait long enough, eventually you're likely to spot one secretly watching you from the shadows. As a matter of fact, foxes are more afraid of people than anything else. Which of these foxes looks afraid?

ZEBRA

If you look carefully at zebras, you'll see that the pattern
of black and white is different on each one.
The males, females and the babies all have different patterns.
Which of these zebras has the most stripes?

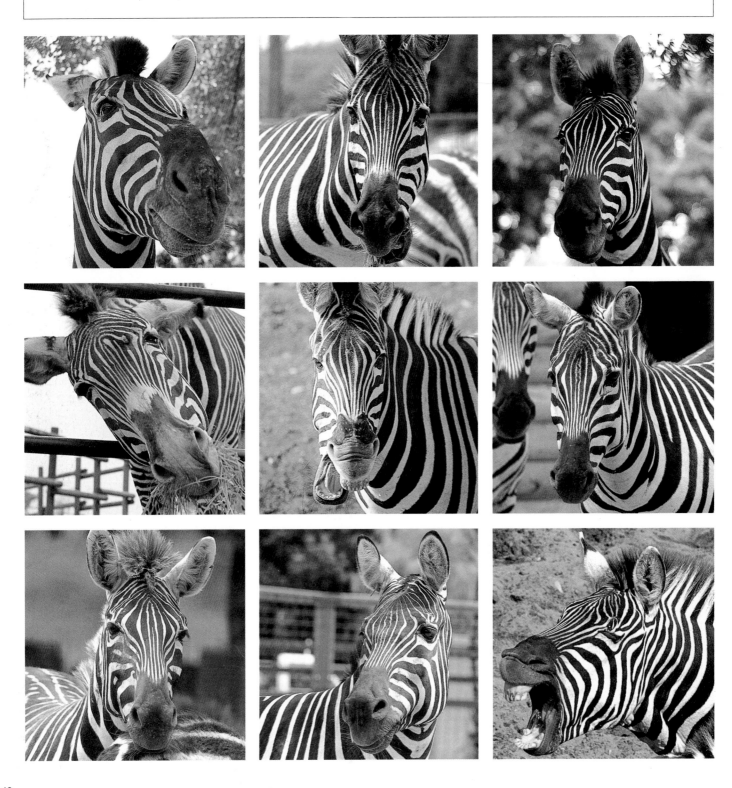

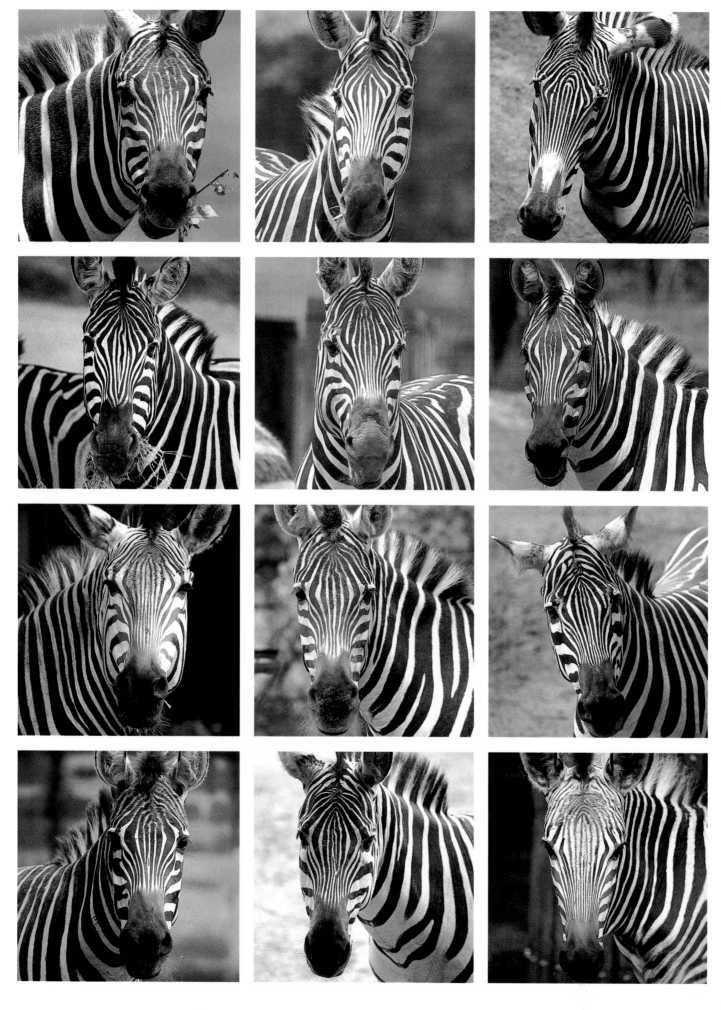

R A C C O O N

Raccoons love sweets. In zoos they'll even sit up and beg
if they see a bag of candy. But if they eat too much of it, they'll
get a stomachache or cavities. So, for the raccoons' sake,
it's better not to give them candy. Do any of these raccoons
look as if they've eaten something they shouldn't have?

LION

Lions love to take naps. And it's not just lions in zoos. Wild lions, too, take naps in the middle of the day, usually in the shade of a tree. So the best time to see them awake at the zoo is in the morning or in the evening. There is one particular feature that distinguishes male lions from females. Can you tell what that is?

JAPANESE MONKEY

Within any group of Japanese monkeys, one will become the leader. The leader gets to eat the best food and to sit in a special seat. But if one gets to be the leader only because of its strength, the others will resent it.
Which of these monkeys look as if they could be a leader?